MW00682261

To:

Sue

From:

Louise

Date:

2004

Message:

to help you
through the
hard times

God's GRACE for tomorrow

Barbara Johnson

God's grace for tomorrow

Copyright © 1986 by Barbara Johnson
Adapted from *Fresh Elastic for Stretched Out Moms*
by Flemming H. Revell, a division of Baker Book House
Company, Grand Rapids, Michigan 49516, U.S.A.

© 2002 Christian Art Gifts, P O Box 1599, Vereeniging,
1930, South Africa

ISBN 1-86920-052-7

Printed in Singapore

02 03 04 05 06 07 08 09 10 11 – 10 9 8 7 6 5 4 3 2 1

The valley of despair

*... we also rejoice in our sufferings,
because we know that suffering
produces perseverance; perseverance
character and character; hope.*
~ Romans 5:3 ~

We all find ourselves in the
valley of despair sometimes. But
I believe we grow in the valley,
because that's where all the
fertilizer is! So learn to welcome the
valley times, and see all the growth
in character that comes from them.

The flowers
of God's grace

His divine power has given us
everything we need for life
and godliness through our
knowledge of him who called us
by his own glory and goodness.
~ 2 Peter 1:3 ~

We can choose to gather to our
hearts the thorns of disappointment,
failure, loneliness, and dismay in our
present situation. Or we can gather the
flowers of God's grace, boundless love,
abiding presence, and unmatched
joy. I choose to gather the flowers.

The journey
to wholeness

Brothers, I do not consider myself
yet to have taken hold of it. But
one thing I do: Forgetting what is
behind and straining toward what is
ahead, I press on toward the goal to
win the prize for which God has called
me heavenward in Christ Jesus.
~ Philippians 3:13-14 ~

We are all on the journey
to wholeness. Some are
farther down the road, some
have stopped at resting places,
and some have even detoured.
But none of us have arrived!

7

The garden of your mind

Finally, brothers, whatever is true,
whatever is noble, whatever is right,
whatever is pure, whatever is lovely, whatever
is admirable – if anything is excellent or
praiseworthy – think about such things.
~ Philippians 4:8 ~

Remember the nursery rhyme,
"Mary, Mary, quite contrary, how
does your garden grow?" How about the
garden of your mind? You can let
weeds sprout and multiply,
let them choke out new life.
Or you can cultivate the
garden of your mind and watch
your days bloom one by one.

8

A sense of humor

Rejoice in the LORD and be glad, you righteous; sing, all you who are upright in heart!
~ Psalm 32:11 ~

Having a sense of humor is what has saved me from the pits. I still get there, but I don't stay there. You have to learn to develop a sturdy ladder to climb out of the pits – one rung at a time, probably. Laughter and humor are the bottom rungs on which to start the upward climb!

The spirit of fun

*Sing, O Daughter of Zion; shout
aloud, O Israel! Be glad and
rejoice with all your heart ...*
~ Zephaniah 3:14 ~

The value of fun lies in the spirit of it,
whether it is climbing windmills, or
marching in a parade, or going up on
the down escalator. Break out of your
little plastic mold and become a real
dingy person (not din-gee, but ding-ee),
even if people think you are fresh
out of a rubber room. Laughing helps.
It's like jogging on the inside.

The great stirring

*Consider how the lilies grow. They do
not labor or spin. Yet I tell you, not even
Solomon in all his splendor was dressed like
one of these. If that is how God clothes the
grass of the field, which is here today, and
tomorrow is thrown into the fire, how much
more will he clothe you, O you of little faith!*
~ Luke 12:27-28 ~

April is rakes, forks, spades, and
lawn mowers on the sidewalk in front
of the hardware store. It is rain
on the weekends, mud on the
kitchen floor, and dirt
and grass stains on the
knees of blue jeans.
April is the great stirring,
the doorway to May.

Gifts to cherish

Fathers, do not exasperate your children; instead, bring them up in the training and instruction of the Lord.
~ Ephesians 6:4 ~

Children are not properties to
own and rule over. They are
gifts to cherish and care for. Our
children are our most important guests.
They enter into our home, ask for
careful attention, stay for a while,
and then leave to follow their own way.

Letting God

Cast all your anxiety on him
because he cares for you.
~ 1 Peter 5:7 ~

We have to give our children to
God and then take our hands off.
It is like wrapping a package up
and putting on a label, and then being
able to send it, without our special
directions of where to go, but
letting God put the address on
the label – or on that life.

Being a mother

*Love is patient, love is kind. It does
not envy, it does not boast, it is not
proud. It always protects, always trusts,
always hopes, always perseveres.*
~ *1 Corinthians 13:4, 7* ~

You know you are a mother when:
 – you have an assortment of
seventeen handmade ashtrays,
and no one in your family smokes.
 – your three-year-old calls you
into the bathroom to retrieve the
Star Wars soldier out of the toilet.
– your freezer is packed with the twenty-
seven boxes of Girl Scout cookies your
daughter couldn't sell to anybody else.

Cleaning out

Have mercy on me, O God ...
blot out my transgressions.
Wash away all my iniquity
and cleanse me from my sin.
~ Psalm 51:1-2 ~

May is a time for cleaning out
drawers, putting fresh paper on
shelves, dumping collections of
junk we have squirreled away.
Clever housekeepers keep an
unused dust mop to shake
out the front door. Then
they shake the real one
out the back door at night.

Never give up hope

*Now it is God who has ... given
us the Spirit as a deposit,
guaranteeing what is to come.
Therefore we are always confident ...*
~ 2 Corinthians 5:5-6 ~

We can never give up hope
with our children. God is not
finished with them or us yet, and
our hope can sometimes mean the
difference between a relationship
that fades away to nothing and a
restoration between parent and child.

Hoping even when

*In this world you will
have trouble. But take heart!
I have overcome the world.*
~ John 16:33 ~

Yes, we can hope even when
we don't see any tangible results
in our relationship with our child.
We don't know what God might be
doing for him or her. We don't know how
God is using what we try to do for him or
her, even when we don't see the results.

All acts of love bear fruit

Let us not become weary in doing
good, for at the proper time we will
reap a harvest if we do not give up.
~ Galatians 6:9 ~

Often we cannot see the
fruits of our work, and so think
our work has been in vain. In
God's service somewhere all our
acts of love bear fruit,
and some heart receives
their blessing and joy.

My name on
the invitation

Come to me, all you who are weary
and burdened, and I will give you rest.
~ Matthew 11:28 ~

RSVP
Christ said, "Come unto me,
All ye that labour
And are heavy laden
And I will give you rest."
These were just
beautiful words to me –
no more – until
I realized that
my name was on
the invitation.

19

Happiness is possible

May the God of hope fill you
with all joy and peace as you trust
in him, so that you may overflow with
hope by the power of the Holy Spirit.
~ Romans 15:13 ~

Happiness and hope are
so closely intertwined
that it seems as though if
we just grab onto that little
bit of hope, it pulls us up
out of the pit enough to
remember that
happiness is possible.

The comforting
arms of God

So with you: Now is your
time of grief, but I will see you
again and you will rejoice, and no
one will take away your joy.
~ John 16:22 ~

My prayer for you is that you will
feel the comforting arms of God
around you, giving you hope
for the future. God can
take your trouble and change
it into a treasure. Your sorrow
can be exchanged for joy,
not just a momentary
smile, but a deep, new joy.

A spirit of pardon

Humble yourselves, therefore,
under God's mighty hand, that
he may lift you up in due time.
Cast all your anxiety on him
because he cares for you.
~ 1 Peter 5:6-7 ~

Offer yourself to God and ask
for a spirit of pardon so your being
will be restored. Tears and sorrow
come, but each time God will be
there to remind you that He cares.

Think about
such things

*... we take captive every thought
to make it obedient to Christ.*
~ 2 Corinthians 10:5 ~

Finally, brothers, whatever is true,
whatever is noble, whatever is
right, whatever is pure, whatever is lovely,
whatever is admirable –
if anything is excellent or praiseworthy –
think about such things.
~ Philippians 4:8 NIV ~

If you have hope

For everything that was written
in the past was written to teach us,
so that through endurance and
the encouragement of the
Scriptures we might have hope.
~ Romans 15:4 ~

To have hope is to be a winner.
Even when you are last in the race,
even when all of your friends'
children are models of perfection
and spiritual holiness while yours
have bitterly disappointed you, you
can be a winner if you have hope.

Victory through hope

*However, I consider my life worth
nothing to me, if only I may
finish the race and complete the task
the Lord Jesus has given me ...*
~ Acts 20:24 ~

Your child is in God's hands –
let Him take the burden
of your sorrow and build victory
through your hope. This isn't
the end of your life. It's the
beginning of your future.

Springs of living water

Everyone who drinks this water
will be thirsty again, but whoever
drinks the water I give him will never
thirst. Indeed, the water I give him
will become in him a spring of
water welling up to eternal life.
~ John 4:13-14 ~

God can give you springs of
living water that will bubble up
from within you like joy
that is percolating from
inside you and bubbling
up to refresh others around you.

Sparkling jewels from God

The wild animals honor me,
the jackals and the owls, because
I provide water in the desert and
streams in the wasteland, to give
drink to my people, my chosen.
~ Isaiah 43:20 ~

Have you ever been in the desert
at night and seen the glistening
stars twinkle brightly? All around
us we can find sparkling jewels
from God scattered in our dark
places – if only we look for them.

ɟ without sorrow

want to know Christ and the
power of his resurrection and the
fellowship of sharing in his sufferings,
becoming like him in his death,
and so, somehow, to attain to
the resurrection from the dead.
~ Philippians 3:10-11 ~

There is no oil without squeezing
the olives, no wine without pressing
the grapes, no fragrance
without crushing the
flowers, and no real
joy without sorrow.

Little gestures

... respect those who work hard
among you, who are over you in
the Lord and who admonish you.
Hold them in the highest regard
in love because of their work ...
~ 1 Thessalonians 5:12-13 ~

Most discouraged people do
not need professional help;
they need those little appreciations,
approvals, or admirations that
can lift their spirits and give
them courage to keep on coping with
the nitty-gritty of life.

Hope deferred

Against all hope, Abraham
in hope believed and so became
the father of many nations ...
~ Romans 4:18 ~

After you have given your
problem to God, you can then
sit back and expect him to
work on it. Giving your burden
to God is where faith comes
in, and hope is always in the
picture, even if it is hope deferred.

A much-needed boost

So then, just as you received
Christ Jesus as Lord, continue
to live in him, rooted and built
up in him, strengthened in the
faith as you were taught,
and overflowing with thankfulness.
~ Colossians 2:6-7 ~

Hope and miracles are almost
synonymous. Sometimes our hope
seems to invite God to do a miracle
in our lives. Sometimes our hope
gets a much-needed boost from a
miracle sent just for that purpose.

Cast your hurt on him

No, in all these things we
are more than conquerors
through him who loved us.
~ Romans 8:37 ~

Lord, give me strength today.
Place within me the ability to cast
my hurt onto you. You have already
borne all of the hurt. You bore it on Calvary. You have fought the sin battle, and
You won the victory. Because of Calvary,
this victory is mine ... Now ... Today.

Learn from mistakes

When you were dead in your sins
and in the uncircumcision of your
sinful nature, God made you alive with
Christ. He forgave us all our sins ...
~ Colossians 2:13 ~

We have failed in many areas
of our lives, but failing doesn't
make us failures! We have to
learn from our mistakes, and learn
how to prevent them in the future.

Your attitude makes the difference!

And he who searches our hearts
knows the mind of the Spirit, because
the Spirit intercedes for the saints
in accordance with God's will.
~ Romans 8:27 ~

August is dedicated to everyone
who is battling for weight or age control.
Remember, no matter how old or
how heavy you are, no matter how
successful or not your diet is, your
attitude makes the difference!

Tap into a
boundless fountain

*A happy heart makes
the face cheerful, but
heartache crushes the spirit.*
~ Proverbs 15:13 ~

Inject some humor into your life!
There are so many ways to do it.
By letting ourselves become children
again, we can tap into a boundless
fountain within us, learning
to laugh all over again. Kids
laugh out of sheer joy; they
don't need a good "reason".

Growing older

Keep yourselves in God's love as you
wait for the mercy of our Lord Jesus
Christ to bring you to eternal life.
~ Jude verse 21 ~

How to tell you are growing older:
– You feel like the night before,
and you haven't been anywhere.
– You know all the answers,
but nobody asks you the questions.
– You turn out the lights for economic
reasons instead of romantic ones.
– You stop looking forward to
your next birthday.

Parental consolation

Rather, as servants of God we
commend ourselves in every way:
in great endurance; in troubles,
hardships and distresses ...
~ 2 Corinthians 6:4 ~

Thoughts to console parents whose
kids have already moved back in:
– Now that the kids are back, you don't
have to eat leftovers. There aren't any.

– Remember when you worried
because you didn't know where your
children were? Now,
you know. They're back
in their own rooms.

       – Before they left, the
       kids were deductible.
       Now, they're just taxing.

Leave the rest
to the Lord

For everything that was written
in the past was written to teach us,
so that through endurance
and the encouragement of the
Scriptures we might have hope.
~ Romans 15:4 ~

Being overweight is no excuse to
check out of life and give up.
Work at your weight the
best you can, leave the rest up
to the Lord, and learn to treat your
weight problem with humor. It will
help, and even though it doesn't
burn very many calories to laugh,
it does make dieting more enjoyable.

Building and remembering

*The fruit of the righteous is a tree of
life, and he who wins souls is wise.*
~ Proverbs 11:30 ~

In our calendar of recovery,
September is our month for building
and remembering the experiences
our children will carry with them throughout
their lives it is a necessary part of growing
up, and a necessary part of a parent's
reflections on all of the
precious yesterdays he
or she shared with a child
who is, perhaps, estranged
and far away today.

The ways to show love

Be devoted to one another
in brotherly love. Honor one
another above yourselves.
~ Romans 12:10 ~

Many are the ways to show love.
A positive reinforcement stated,
a note written, a diaper changed,
a meal cooked, a soft word spoken,
a tub of dirty clothes washed,
a pat of reassurance given,
a kiss of unrestrained passion shared,
a car repaired, a flower sent,
a loving spirit lived!

He is mine

I give them eternal life, and
they shall never perish; no one can
snatch them out of my hand.
~ John 10:28 ~

One day a father was talking
to a friend about his son, who had
caused great heartache. The friend
said, "If he were my son, I would
kick him out." The father thought for a
moment, then said, "Yes, if he were
your son, so would I. But he is not your
son; he is mine and I can't do it."

Love protects,
trusts and hopes

*And over all these virtues
put on love, which binds them
all together in perfect unity.*
~ *Colossians 3:14* ~

Love always:
Protects
— I want to take the hurt for my child.
Instead, I will protect and love him.
Trusts
— I trust, even when my
husband travels a lot and
faces life's temptations.
Hopes
— We still share our
dreams for life together.

No strings attached

*Be kind and compassionate to
one another; forgiving each other,
just as in Christ God forgave you.*
~ Ephesians 4:32 ~

Face your child, forgive him
or her, love him, and welcome
him with open arms. You
might even get hurt again,
but you don't have to agree with
your child, just to love her
and reassure her of your love,
which is as unconditional as that
of God – no strings attached.

I have my God

God blessed them and said to them,
"Be fruitful and increase in number;
fill the earth and subdue it ..."
Genesis 1:28

Would I have been better off if
I had never married, had never had
children? ... No! In spite of all the
tragedy, and all the heartache, and
all the sorrow, I wouldn't trade my life
for any other life in the world. I have
the laughter to remind me of the good
times, and I have my God, who gives
me the strength to survive the
tragedy, and the joy to
appreciate my blessings!

God's grace and love are sufficient

But he said to me, "My grace is sufficient for you, for my power is made perfect in weakness."
~ 2 Corinthians 12:9 ~

The encouragement I can give you for October is to remember that God's grace and love are sufficient for any situation you could ever experience. God will listen to your fears and assure you that He is in control.

Based in the love of God

It [love] is not rude, it is not self-seeking, it is not easily angered, it keeps no record of wrongs. Love never fails ...
~ 1 Corinthians 13:5, 8 ~

My family and I know we love each other. We know that our love, based in the love of God, has withstood the test and is stronger than ever. No matter what happens, we love each other, no strings attached.

With you during the trial

Do not be anxious about anything,
but in everything, by prayer and
petition, with thanksgiving, present your
requests to God. And the peace
of God, which transcends all
understanding, will guard your
hearts and your minds in Christ Jesus.
~ Philippians 4:6-7 ~

Nothing comes into the life of
a Christian that God doesn't know
about. Then you can just relax
and kick it out of gear for a
while and know that God
will be with you during the trial.

Into the healing stage

This is the confidence we
have in approaching God:
that if we ask anything according
to his will, he hears us.
~ 1 John 5:14 ~

When "Whatever, Lord!"
replaces "Why me?" then you can
know that you are on the way to
growing through your trial. You
are finally into the healing stage. You
have survived the panic situation, and
you are moving into normalcy again.